Hands' Desire

poems by

Michael Beebe

Finishing Line Press
Georgetown, Kentucky

Hands' Desire

Copyright © 2021 by Michael Beebe
ISBN 978-1-64662-399-0 First Edition
All rights reserved under International and Pan-American Copyright Conventions. No part of this book may be reproduced in any manner whatsoever without written permission from the publisher, except in the case of brief quotations embodied in critical articles and reviews.

ACKNOWLEDGMENTS

"Mottainai" was published, in a slightly different version, in the 2011 *Marin Poetry Center Anthology*

Publisher: Leah Huete de Maines

Editor: Christen Kincaid

Cover Art: Michael Beebe

Author Photo: Michael Beebe

Cover Design: Elizabeth Maines McCleavy

Order online: www.finishinglinepress.com
       also available on amazon.com

Author inquiries and mail orders:
Finishing Line Press
PO Box 1626
Georgetown, Kentucky 40324
USA

Table of Contents

I

Mottainai 1
Ad for a Sewing Machine 2
Picture of the Bride and Groom 3
Antonello's St. Jerome 4
Accedia 5
Hands' Desire 6

II

Political Poem 9
Kant and Freud 10
Feeding the Quail 11
The Afternoon is Late, and the Light is Old 12
Well-Articulated Before All Description 13
Right There, All There 14

III

Tonight and Again Tomorrow 17
The Falling Rain, the Slant of Light 18
Marine Layer 19
Mountain Home Road 20
I Came Out of the Dirt 21
Last Notes of the Organ as the Recital Ends 22

IV

Dear Brother 25
Getting Up at Night to Pee 26
One Expects to Awaken 27
The Shapes of the Days Don't Say 28
I Will Die Before I Learn 29
My Notebooks 30

I

Mottainai

When the truth of it
settles around you like
the clench of the pattern
in an ocean-worn rock

broken and surf-tossed
into its shape and smooth
curve until come to some
distinct human significance

Or when the warp and weft is
age and use and wear and fade
clothes patched and quilted
wood shaped into a tool

made by hand and used by hand
meaning set deep into the stuff
so it glows there before you
in its hard-worn beauty

Ad for a Sewing Machine, 1909

I'm looking, puzzled, at a picture
of a young woman shown there in a
sewing machine ad from a century ago.
I suppose the one hundred years gone
is the reason I cannot for the moment
see that she is beautiful—
although of course she must have been,
or been thought to be,
else why put her in an ad?

But then, cognitive leap,
I do see her, and she is beautiful,
and I am suddenly happy.

Picture of the Bride and Groom

The couple stands on a balcony with the greens
and sunlight of summer framing their good faces.
They are smiling out of the picture at us, happy
but a little frightened, husband and wife, new-made.
We are there too, unphotographed, standing behind
the camera, smiling, clapping our good wishes,
supporters, friends, parents, family, linked by the
shared strong emotions of love, and duty, and care.

We find these occasions, to pledge ourselves
to the bride and groom, their new life, and also
again to each other, for we know it can only be so.
The construction of our lives is complicated past
understanding, a novel only a god could write,
but none did, it is ours, and we make it together.

Antonello's St. Jerome

Antonello's St. Jerome is given to us distanced
and formal, his palazzo classical and splendid.
We are shown the saint sitting intent at his desk
in his studiolo, where the artistically opened
wall directs the sun to fall brilliant and slant,
lighting the book he is reading. We see him
as the painter sees him, a man for such a room,
for such a civilized and civilizing place.

Not in fact true to the saint, who was not much
interested in civilizing. Rather see him barefoot
in dirt and animal skins, ranting in the wilderness.
Rather see Antonello himself in the saint's study,
there among the books, telling us what he knows
of scholarship, and thought, and a place to read.

Accedia

"The real disillusionment" you said, "is seeing that
enlightenment is real, the good life should be lived,
duty and care are required of the rational being,
seeing that's all true and then feeling no different."

We were drinking beer and it wasn't late yet
but it would be. We were sitting in your study,
we should have been working but we weren't,
we were talking and doubting and drinking beer.

"You know the answer to that," I said. "You told me
last year when we were reading the medievals.
If we were monks we'd be punished. Accedia is a sin."

But we weren't monks, only graduate students
and we had to find for ourselves any presence.
"Have another beer" was all you said.

Hands' Desire

The thing bright in imagination and desire
and the passion of the new beginning
held in potential in the hands is a love
so old it is in the muscle-memory.

The part of me in my hands speaks to me,
urgent, saying plant, make, build.
My hands have strength to grip though less,
even old hands still fit to the tool's handle.

Yet my soul is tired, as if sleeping
I lost forever the comfort of sleep.
A new morning refreshes me somewhat

but it is the world reborn, not I.
Hands' desire doesn't end but the soul wavers,
the loss lingers, and is not explained.

II

Political Poem

In order to understand how tolerance is a virtue,
consider sitting at table with a cousin or uncle
or even brother, who professes some religion
or ideology negative, alien, utterly unbelievable
to you and the tenets of which, if implemented,
would coerce from you your self-regard and
your rights and force you to be another person.
So if you and he cannot find how to disagree
and then move on to the weather
                                            you will find
that in the end you can only move on to the
argument under arms. For tolerance is a virtue
that really only works well reciprocally, and
when you realize that, your sense of the essential
orderability of things now weakens further.

Kant and Freud

We all used to think that Freud told us
deep and important things about the self.
But as you live with it, you find his
ghostly actors and intricate inner structures

either absent ghosts or, for some sufferers,
haunting alien presences. But alien,
other, not-you, and having nothing to do
with your own fragile sense of self.

So Kant begins to seem "practical".
Contra Hume, he assures you of your self,
determinate and metaphysically distinct,
secure in a transcendental unity.

But a formal unity merely, since on bad days
all that means is, the less unity the less self.

Feeding the Quail

The day began in rain and so the quail
did not venture out until later, becoming
hungry I suppose. When they did come
the rain had stopped and they ate happily,
occasionally standing up on tip-toe
to flap their wings briskly, drying off
it seemed, looking cheerful sure. I watched,
looking up from my philosophy book.

It will rain again soon, winter is almost here.
Mild, here in California, but the leaves color
and fall, we need an extra blanket nights and
mornings it is dark late and evenings early.
The year turns, but it is anyway a person's
clear duty to feel the good of the good.

The Afternoon Is Late, and the Light Is Old

Wind is always about distance, and time's passing.
All day yesterday and all day today the wind
pushed and lifted and pressed the tree branches,
making them rustle and hum but then shred and clash.
And the line of the roof-tree against the distant blue
of the far and grayed sky—the afternoon is late
and the light is old, and sad, and cannot sustain life.
We see our deaths plainly before us in this light.

Wind is always about distance and time's passing,
so here near some end we are thankful that it is
the day that ends, thank the earth's clock that
says the closing of the day has come, as it does,
bringing us calm for the night and with the old,
warm comfort of sleep, hope again in the morning.

Well-Articulated Before All Description

Dawn's growing light thickens shadow
into thing. Cold colors suffusing, diffuse
but brightening. Black line of fence-row,
curb and path and eave, homely shapes

of garden tree and shed and house
mark no particular significance but
the world's entirely unhuman presence.
We may look, but what we see does not

do fair by all this, things quite separate
from us. Were we to see truer, we would
acknowledge a plainer being than that

which bears the burden of our intentions
and our hearts, but calm, substantial,
well-articulated before all description.

Right There, All There

Padding along barefoot at night
on the way to turn down the heat,
feet familiar through dark rooms

and I think that's all I'm doing—
but it's the embrace of all this, touch
of feet, known planes of lighter darkness

into darker shadow, rectangles and
cubes of rooms, felt densities of
volumes of space in deeper shadow.

Then the sudden sharp small enthusiasm
as of some intense and interesting new thing,
the sense of the amazing possibility of it.

And for that moment all at once it is
right there, all there, clear and bright.

III

Tonight and Again Tomorrow

It was late, tonight, before
the tension eased in my chest and
I could sit, quiet finally, give over
work and acknowledge day's end,

able, although tomorrow would be
much the same as today,
to make a moderate peace
with the days before, the day

after. For it is wrong, I know,
to give tension of such a dubious basis
houseroom, even though

it will all begin again tomorrow
despite what I do,
or think, or where I go.

The Falling Rain, the Slant of Light

Today I don't know what I'm doing,
I don't know what comes next.
I stand dazzled in the sun in the morning,
wet and blank in the rain falling soft
in the afternoon, and if there weren't
something in me that knows what to do
I would stand stricken, emptied to a
pure vacancy. But somebody is here
who does know how to do things and he
takes charge and finds the plan of the day.
I don't know him but I need him. I think
I would fail again and again to deduce my
tasks from the falling rain, the slant of light,
the sun moving across the earth's face.

Marine Layer

Crows cawing long and harsh and wild,
holding hard and swaying wide, high
in wind-driven tree tops back-lit black
on the dull white sky at the end of the day.
Sea wind sharp with redwood and bay,
pungent bright-bitter herbal green scents
as of messages we know but cannot read,
and the old, cold salt smell of the sea.

Wind increasing, fog from the ocean darks
the deeps of the valleys, veils the hills.
Last sun in the west fades, fades more,
shadows fall heavy on the hills' east slopes.
Fast-streaming cloud, rising rough hand of the wind,
the self-indexical gray and meaning light.

Mountain Home Road

It was always raining,
the black firs covering
the hills behind the house,
the mountains always there
at the edge of the sky to the east,
and I'd be waiting in the rain,
the rain and gray light,
waiting for the yellow bus
to come rumbling down the hill.
The bus door would open
and the bus driver, sometimes
comforting, mostly alien
and frightening because
distantly, indifferently adult.
And I would get on the school bus.

The poorer children from the houses
on the poorer land up the hill
would be in the bus already,
smelling of wet wool, wet shoes
and the unwashed young bodies
that yet smelled less strongly, less
intrusively than the adults whose
weekly-washed sexual bodies
smelled so distinctively to me
then hairless and small, terrifying,
and of some other place where
people went when they got older,
did not talk the same anymore,
new words, a different knowledge.

I Came Out of the Dirt

I came out of the dirt.
When I first looked around
it was raining but the
next time I looked the
sun was warm on grass
and there were flowers.

I lived with my family
and we lived on a farm
and the farm was near a
town, and we knew
many people in the town.
I worked on the farm.

I was a farm boy and I
plowed fields and cared
for cows and chickens and
walked in the woods in the rain.
I came out of the dirt
and I looked around.

I came out of the dirt.
Days when it rains are truest
because then it is easier to
find the view from the dirt
and there one always
begins again and asks.

Last Notes of the Organ as the Recital Ends

It can happen,
sometime, that you
have a powerful insight
that is yet so painful
you can only bow your
head before that truth as it
speaks itself in the voice of a god
yet in some human tongue
so that we may understand
inaudible but resonant
echoing, the last notes
of the organ as the
recital ends

IV

Dear Brother,

Today I read, and wrote, and thought,
then walked and looked. And now I sit and rest,
think about you and begin to write this note.
It rained last night and through the window
while I slept I heard the rain falling slow
and heavy-steady. This morning the ground
is so saturated that surface water sparkles
and the palm tree looks vividly green.
It is wet where you are in Oregon, I know,
but possibly not yet so new and green,
being more northerly. It would be good
to meet and talk. I am struggling with
my work again, finding no words, and
no voice that appeals; but philosophy
is wonderfully exciting for me now.
I know how you will be laughing, say
"Then why didn't you study harder in
graduate school?" And I will smile shame-
facedly, granting your point. But maybe
it's the attraction of studying on one's own,
or maybe the onset of old age is making much
less relevant but philosophy more dear.
I don't know but I would hear your voice, debate
your thought, deliberate your question, sit
with you to talk. Someday soon, I expect,
although right now in my days things go well,
I feel strong enough. But soon, I know, soon
again in the realm of the merely possible,
after my sojourn, that one you never made.

Getting Up at Night to Pee

Getting up at night to pee
I'm thinking of my grandfather,
old farmer, always took a little
pee can to put under his bed,
never quite trusted himself to
late-come indoor plumbing.
My eyes track down the long line,
my desk through dining room to kitchen,
along the kitchen counters,
ending at the sink now dark
with night's blind window.
Think how these shapes, so familiar,
represent a certain late 20th
century kitchen concept—
That I like, but my grandmother
would have blinked and sniffed,
doubting the aesthetic of stainless steel.
My mother, well, she would have smiled
to look where I live;
and my other grandmother
would have snorted at the escape
from work it all represented,
too easy she would think,
angry old woman.
Me, though, I push all these shades
back to shade, think merely it is
my kitchen in the middle of the night,
think how I must just
go back to bed, no good coming
of middle-of-the-night
kitchen visits no matter what
some stray impulse to remember
one's past might sign, think it's
just night and I just got up to pee,
think it's late already, and they're
long dead now, and I'm old.

One Expects to Awaken

At home one expects to awaken in
comfort of familiarity, accumulated
meanings serving the intended purpose
of amplifying self. But one also expects,
or fears, that from the amplification
one will be able to look long enough
to see one more frame of that mystery
one fears, but to which one is bound by
those same definitions, that same syntax,
from which I came too, and you:
mysterious, and no longer home-like, either.

Some mornings it is only the world.
Other mornings the world has cracks,
or maybe vistas, so to speak.
We can try to look, but being mere creatures
never know what we see, or even that,
until far later you awaken in the night,
suddenly thinking some thought
you can barely articulate, that tears you so
you scream silently. Or maybe then
settling enough to think, to think
this new thing that you yet cannot.

The Shapes of the Days Don't Say

Here am I, still trying, earnest and
clumsy in my intentness and my
mistakes. And why should the world
notice? It does not. Nor is that what
unsettles me, causes second and third
thoughts, now and on many days,
at the end of the day when
whatever has been, or been done,
has been, and what has not hangs there,
seen somehow but in practice unnamable.
The shapes of the days don't say.

That is why any day can become
something that you find yourself in
and are yet unable to tell where that is:
where that is, when you might have
thought you knew; where that is,
when at the end of any day the map
of the moments would surely say;
where that is when if, we think,
we look truly we would surely know.
Though we do not and, with a kind
of weariness, come to doubt all. Yet
why should we expect ever to know?
Nor do we, and the days pass, and
each day one tries, and so time passes.

I Will Die Before I Learn

As I explained to her, so young,
it was a poem about age, and
growing old, and what that means
and all that changes; but she
just looked puzzled, and so
we moved on to other things

I will die before I learn what
anything means I say in fear
and a kind of sickish shame.
It was one of those moments
when you come back to the
same things again, all the psychic
knots, all the ordinary human
stuff, the conflicts, paradoxes,
puzzles, and the plain dumb
miseries you've thought about
however many times before.

And so you feel defeated
and slightly nauseated.
You try to disavow the
duty, but don't get far.
You don't believe you can,
or should. It's your life,
all the conflicts, all
the curious memories,
how you can't seem to
find any clear meaning,
no recognizable self, and
it all presses so hard, all
the formless pain, all the
muddled, hapless clutter.

My Notebooks

Each time I write in my notebooks now
I wonder whether I will have time
to dispose of them all before I die;
or whether I will have the courage,
or even want to. Why, I ask,
should I take on that task?
Let whoever comes to clean out
my house do it, throw them out
along with my old clothes, there's
nothing about either of them that's
valuable, or embarrassing, or personal, even.
Working journals, that's all they are,
no more significant, after, than old shoes.
Easy for the housekeeper to throw out,
harder for my wife, who loves me.
But now I see I will after all do the self-
indulgent thing I wanted to do anyway.
I'm sorry, dear. They don't matter,
old shoes, that's all. I love you.

Michael Beebe came to poetry later in life. Sometime in his fifties he found that poetry was the only thing he could read, nothing else, he felt, was suitably serious, beautiful and truth-apt all together, nothing else adequate to express all that needed to be said. He reports that he had ceased to be able to read novels some years before, and now history and biography and essays were failing him: but he discovered poetry. So, after a number of years of intense reading, he began attempting to write poems of his own. Michael earned a BSc in Physics, a PhD in Philosophy, taught Philosophy for a few years on temporary contracts, and then became a CPA to earn a living. He spent a number of years first in audit and then in consulting with Deloitte, one of the remaining large CPA firms. He finished his career as Vice President of Business Services at Santa Rosa Junior College, in California. While he lived in California, he was a member of the Marin Poetry Center, an organization devoted to poetry and poets, and he wishes to thank that organization for all it offered an engaged, amateur poet. He now lives in retirement with his wife in the Portland, Oregon area. He reads philosophy and poetry, and works at his writing.

www.ingramcontent.com/pod-product-compliance
Lightning Source LLC
LaVergne TN
LVHW041507070426
835507LV00012B/1377